D0821804

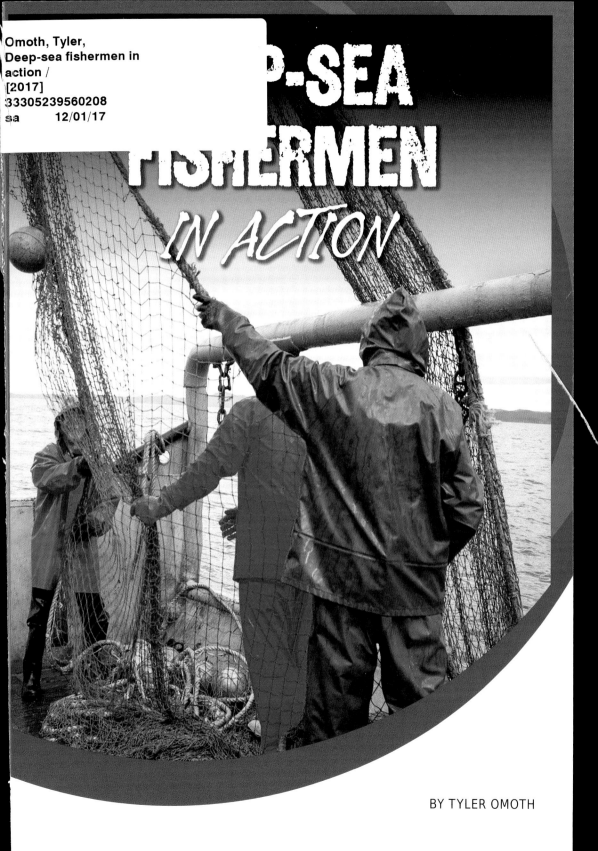

DEEP-SEA FISHERMEN
IN ACTION

Omoth, Tyler,
Deep-sea fishermen in
action /
[2017]
33305239560208
sa   12/01/17

BY TYLER OMOTH

The Child's World®
childsworld.com

Published by The Child's World®
1980 Lookout Drive • Mankato, MN 56003-1705
800-599-READ • www.childsworld.com

Photographs ©: DoublePhoto Studio/Shutterstock Images, cover, 1, 14, 22; SolStock/iStockphoto, 5; Andreas G. Karelias/Shutterstock Images, 6; U.S. Coast Guard District 17, 8, 9; Petty Officer 2nd Class Grant DeVuyst/U.S. Coast Guard District 17, 11; Andrej Pol/Shutterstock Images, 12; Neil Annenberg/Shutterstock Images, 16; Shutterstock Images, 18, 26, 28; David Peter Robinson/Shutterstock Images, 19; iStockphoto, 20; Andrew Vaughan/ The Canadian Press/AP Images, 24; Karoline Cullen/Shutterstock Images, 25

Copyright © 2017 by The Child's World®
All rights reserved. No part of this book may be reproduced or utilized in any form or by any means without written permission from the publisher.

ISBN 9781503816282

LCCN 2016945658

Printed in the United States of America
PA02320

TABLE OF
CONTENTS

FAST FACTS 4

Chapter 1
ABANDON SHIP 7

Chapter 2
TANGLED 15

Chapter 3
MEN OVERBOARD 23

Think About It 29
Glossary 30
To Learn More 31
Selected Bibliography 31
Index 32

FAST FACTS

What's the Job?

- Deep-sea fishermen go out to some of the most dangerous parts of the world's oceans. They catch popular seafood such as tuna, crab, and **scallops**.

- There is no formal education for the job. But many deep-sea fishermen grow up around fishermen. They learn the trade from more experienced fishermen.

The Dangers

- Deep-sea fishing can involve injuries from tools and equipment on the deck of the ship.

- Falling overboard and being on a capsizing ship are also serious dangers.

Important Stats

- In 2014, there were 22 fishing-related deaths in the United States.

- The average commercial fisherman makes $59,000 per year. That can vary a lot based on how many fish are caught and what rank the fisherman holds. Captains earn more than the deckhands who help maintain the ship.

Chapter 1

ABANDON SHIP

It was a blustery night in June 2015. Fishing boat captain Steve Berry was monitoring an incoming storm. His boat, the *Kupreanof*, was traveling near Cape Fairweather in the Gulf of Alaska.

Steve and his three-person crew were headed for salmon fishing grounds in Bristol Bay. The *Kupreanof* was 73 feet (22 m) long. The boat had been out of service for nearly 20 years. But now it was at sea again and facing a difficult test. The **radar** showed a storm heading toward the boat.

By midnight, high winds and large waves rocked the *Kupreanof*. A few hours later, Steve noticed that his ship was tilting to the side. The waves started to fill the ship with water. At first, the water was running off the deck. But by three o'clock in the morning, the deck of the ship was taking on more and more water.

◀ **Deep-sea fishermen often wear rain gear to protect themselves from the weather.**

▲ Footage from a Coast Guard video shows the *Kupreanof* sinking.

Steve woke his crew. He ordered them to put on their **immersion** suits. These suits are designed to keep people alive in near-freezing water. Steve called **Mayday** on the ship's radio. He and his crew watched the back of the ship dip below the waves. The *Kupreanof* was sinking, and it was going down fast.

While the storm raged on, Steve called on the radio to two nearby fishing boats for help. A rescue from a fishing vessel is very difficult in rough seas. But a rescue was the crew's only chance. Thirty minutes passed. The icy water covered more and more of the *Kupreanof*. If help did not arrive soon, the four fishermen would be floating helplessly in their life raft in their immersion suits.

The Gulf of Alaska typically drops to temperatures of 50 degrees Fahrenheit (10°C) and lower during June. The human body cannot handle such low temperatures for very long. Without a life raft or immersion suits, the fishermen would survive a maximum of six hours in the water. With both safety features available, their chance of survival was much better.

▲ A Coast Guard video shows the crew of the *Kupreanof* in a life raft.

Suddenly, over the howling wind, the sound of a U.S. Coast Guard helicopter reached the fishermen's ears. The Coast Guard has been training rescue swimmers and answering ships' distress calls for many years. Steve contacted them on the radio. He asked them what to do.

Jason Yelvington was the Coast Guard helicopter team's rescue swimmer. He preferred to rescue people from the water or a life raft, not the sinking ship. That's because a sinking ship is unstable and dangerous. So, the crew's best chance for survival was to abandon ship. But Steve told the rescue pilot that he had another problem. One of his crewmen couldn't swim.

Steve instructed the nonswimming crewman to release the life raft and jump directly to it. The *Kupreanof* bobbed and swayed in the water. The man leaped off the boat, landing on the life raft. He clung to it for his life.

The remaining men slid along the ship's railing. They got into a good position to plunge into the frigid water. One by one, they jumped in and began swimming to the life raft as fast as possible.

The helicopter lowered Jason down to the water with a motorized lift. He quickly reached the life raft and helped the first man onto the lift.

**A Coast Guard rescue worker practices ▶
lifting a victim out of the sea.**

Because of the cold temperatures, the rescue swimmer and the fishermen were all struggling to breathe. The ship's diesel fuel was spilling into the water. The fumes made breathing even more difficult.

The wind and the waves battered the men. Jason used his extensive training to get each man safely to the lift. One by one, the fishermen were hoisted up to the helicopter. Just as the last man was lifted into the air, the *Kupreanof* groaned and sank to the bottom of the Gulf of Alaska. The life raft was still attached to the fishing vessel and was dragged down with it.

When the fishermen reached the safety of the Coast Guard helicopter, they finally had time to reflect on the situation. Their boat was sinking in the cold water. They had almost lost their lives.

The evening before the *Kupreanof* set sail, Steve had taken his crew out to eat. After dinner, Steve had told them they needed to do a safety check. Each person had put on his immersion suit so he knew how to do it quickly. They had double-checked the life raft as well. Proper training, the right safety equipment, rescue help, and keeping calm under pressure kept the crew of the *Kupreanof* alive to fish another day.

◄ **An immersion suit can save the life of a deep-sea fisherman.**

Chapter 2

TANGLED

Gareth Jones had been on fishing boats for most of his life. As a child, he went out with his father, who was a commercial fisherman in the United Kingdom. Gareth always dreamed about operating a fishing boat of his own someday.

Gareth achieved his dream when he bought the *Ronan Orla*, a 36-foot (11-m) scallop **dredging** boat. But the boat was expensive. Gareth didn't have enough money left over to pay a crew. He also couldn't afford to keep the boat equipped with all the safety features a commercial fishing boat should have. He owned his boat, but it was a struggle to make a living by himself.

On March 30, 2014, Gareth set out on his boat alone in the Irish Sea, just off the coast of England. He was fishing for scallops. Scallop fishing is always dangerous. The popular shellfish live on the seabed close to shore. That means fishing boats run the risk of hitting large rocks hidden underwater near the shore.

◄ **A deep-sea fishing boat has many moving parts that can be dangerous.**

The scallop boats themselves are loaded with equipment. The dredges are large metal fishing nets. They can weigh up to 2,600 pounds (1,180 kg). Gareth released his nets along the seabed to pick up the scallops that lay there. Later, he used large ropes and chains to lift the dredge out of the water with the help of a large **winch**. The winch turned with powerful force. Gareth knew from experience that if he wasn't careful, he could easily get knocked overboard by his equipment. He also had to be careful not to get caught in the **rigging** or crushed against the rail of the boat by a swinging dredge.

Operating a scallop dredging ship is already dangerous for a well-trained crew. For Gareth, it was a constant challenge. He had to walk on the slippery deck while trying to avoid being hit by the dredge. He also had to avoid being cut by a wire or caught in the machinery.

Gareth started to bring up his catch. The winch hauled up the dredges. The winch spun quickly to bring in the slack rope from the underwater nets. But Gareth got too close to the powerful machinery. He was stuck! Gareth would soon be crushed if he did not get himself free.

Most dredging ships have an emergency shutdown button to stop the machine. They also have a release lever on the winch.

◀ **A fisherman empties the scallops out of his net.**

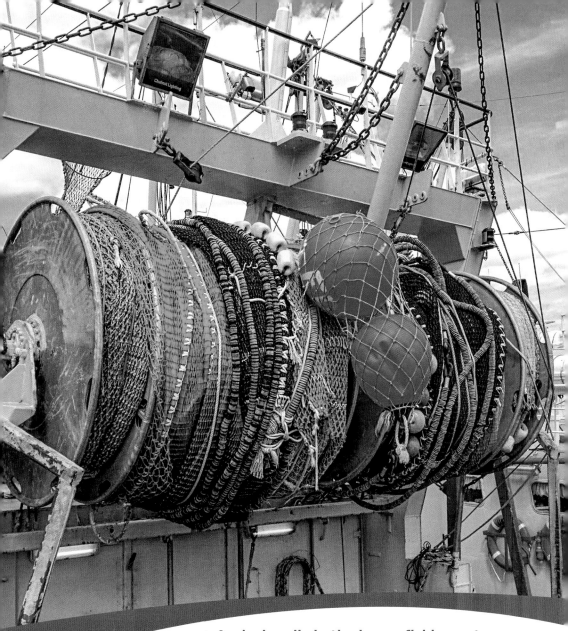

▲ **A winch pulls in the heavy fishing nets.**

But these safety features cost money. Unfortunately, Gareth had not installed either one on his boat. The winch continued to pull Gareth in closer and closer.

At 3:15 p.m., another local fishing boat noticed Gareth's boat and realized it was in danger. The other boat's crew called for emergency assistance. Emergency responders scrambled to get a rescue boat to the location where the *Ronan Orla* drifted.

▲ **An inexpensive fishing boat may cost $100,000 to $150,000.**

Once onboard, the rescue workers saw the battle that had taken place between machine and man. The machinery had overpowered Gareth. The extent of his injuries was severe. The rescue workers decided to call emergency medical crews and a helicopter to meet them on shore. Then they towed the boat back to land.

For Gareth Jones, the price of captaining his own boat was too high. Because he didn't have other crewmembers and the proper safety equipment, he did not survive. He became tangled in the winch and suffered injuries that caused his death.

As a result of this accident, a British organization started a fundraising campaign. The money it raises helps fishermen install the proper safety equipment on their boats. The organization's funds also go toward replacing old and dangerous deck machinery. It's a small step, but one that could make deep-sea fishing a little bit safer for those who brave the oceans each day.

◀ **Working on a fishing boat alone can be very dangerous.**

Chapter 3

MEN OVERBOARD

It was a cold November morning in Nova Scotia, Canada. The sun was not even up yet. But the docks were humming with activity. Nearly 1,500 boats left shore at the same time. The lobster fishermen of Nova Scotia call it Dumping Day. Dumping Day is the start of the lobster-fishing season. All of the captains want their boats to be the first to reach the best fishing spots. Once they reach the spot they want, the crews launch, or "dump," their lobster traps overboard and wait for the big catch.

Boat captains weaved in and out, trying not to hit other boats and shoreline structures. Deckhands worked feverishly to secure all of the cargo on deck so it didn't slide around the slippery surface. Extra Canadian Coast Guard ships kept watch over the area. They were ready to spring into action if there was an accident.

◀ **On Dumping Day, the fishermen of Nova Scotia get started before dawn.**

▲ **Fishing boats crowd the shore on the morning of Dumping Day.**

The *Nomada Queen* was one of the boats that launched from shore on Dumping Day 2015. But the excitement of the first day of lobster season quickly turned into a nightmare.

Nate King, a 24-year-old deckhand, was standing on top of the ship's 270 lobster traps, also known as "pots." Suddenly, a loud snap rang through the air. The pots that he was standing on tumbled overboard and into the ocean. The aluminum railing along the edge of the boat had broken. Much of the boat's equipment, along with two deckhands, fell overboard.

▲ **The Canadian Coast Guard patrols the shores of Nova Scotia on Dumping Day to keep fishermen safe.**

Nate landed among all of the traps and ropes. He quickly realized he was tangled. Something had caught his leg and was dragging him down. He reached for the knife that he kept in his boot. He didn't know what was tangled with his boot, so he cut the boot itself. After a few terrifying moments, the boot fell away. Nate was free but still underwater. He inflated his life vest. Then he swam to get clear of all of the equipment in the water.

Nate had recently taken an emergency training class. He knew that the shock of the cold water would make him want to gasp for air. But if he tried to inhale when he was still below the surface, he would inhale water. Instead, he held his breath and tried to keep calm until his head was back above water. He soon noticed he wasn't the only one in the water.

His coworker, Wayne Atwood, had also fallen overboard. Wayne was panicking and struggling to stay above the water. Nate grabbed Wayne and held him up. Nate struggled to keep Wayne calm and above water. Once Wayne was calm, the pair began to swim away from the ropes and lobster pots. They made their way toward the ship.

Nate's father, Ricky, was the captain of the ship. Ricky was doing what he could to retrieve his men. He had radioed for help, and rescue teams were on the way.

◀ **Lobster pots are big enough to hold several lobsters.**

▲ Life jackets are an essential piece of
safety equipment.

Nate and Wayne continued swimming toward the *Nomada Queen*. The men still onboard lowered ropes from the ship. Nate tied the first rope around Wayne, and the crewmembers lifted him to safety. Soon after, they lifted Nate onboard as well.

Rescue teams arrived. They took Wayne to the hospital. Thanks to his recent emergency training and his life jacket, Nate had survived the ordeal in good shape.

Nate remained with his boat. The *Nomada Queen* lost a lot of equipment and money that day. But it did not lose any of its crew. A Dumping Day disaster had been avoided.

Because of the high number of accidents like this one, the Nova Scotia Labour Department passed a new law. The law requires all commercial fishermen to wear life jackets while working on deck. Several companies have purchased large numbers of life jackets to donate to boats to help the cause.

THINK ABOUT IT

- What would life be like if you were out on the ocean for weeks at a time? Would you enjoy it?
- Can you think of any ways to make deep-sea fishing safer? Would you risk your life to be a deep-sea fisherman?
- In some seasons, deep-sea fishermen may make a lot of money. In other seasons, they may not make much at all. It depends on the number of fish they catch. Would you rather have a career where you can make a small, reliable income? Or would you prefer a job where you might make big money but risk making almost nothing?

GLOSSARY

dredging (DREJ-ing): Dredging means using a net or tool to scrape the seabed for shellfish or other animals. The dredging boat scraped the bottom of the sea to get clams.

immersion (i-MUHR-zhuhn): Immersion means being completely covered by liquid. The immersion suit kept the fisherman warm when he was in the water.

Mayday (MAY-day): Mayday is a universal word for help or emergency. The captain called Mayday over the radio when his ship started to sink.

radar (RAY-dahr): Radar is a method of locating objects by reflecting radio waves off of objects and receiving the reflected waves. The captain saw three other ships on his radar.

rigging (RIG-ing): Rigging is a number of ropes, cables, and chains used on ships to control sails and other operations on deck. The deckhands adjusted the rigging to move the sails when the wind changed.

scallops (SKAL-ups): Scallops are a shellfish with two fan-shaped shells. Scallops live in the ocean, close to shore.

winch (WINCH): A winch is mechanical wheel that winds cable or rope to pull or release heavy objects. The crew used a winch to haul up the heavy nets.

TO LEARN MORE

Books

Gordon, Nick. *Deep Sea Fishermen*. Minneapolis: Bellwether Media, 2013.

Pendergast, George. *Deep-Sea Fishing*. New York: Gareth Stevens Publishing, 2015.

Schwartz, Tina P. *Deep-Sea Fishing*. New York: PowerKids Press, 2012.

Web Sites

Visit our Web site for links about deep-sea fishermen: childsworld.com/links

Note to Parents, Teachers, and Librarians: We routinely verify our Web links to make sure they are safe and active sites. So encourage your readers to check them out!

SELECTED BIBLIOGRAPHY

Cummings, Kathryn. "Safety Campaign Launched Following Death of Fisherman." *Cambrian News*. Tindle Newspapers, 26 Jan. 2016. Web. 7 June 2016.

"Fisherman Washed Overboard on Dumping Day Shares Story." *CTV News Atlantic*. Bell Media, 2 Dec. 2015. Web. 7 June 2016.

Viechnicki, Joe. "Skipper Recounts Sinking on Fairweather Grounds." *KFSK Community Radio*. Narrows Broadcasting Corporation, 10 June 2015. Web. 7 June 2016.

INDEX

Atwood, Wayne, 27–28

Berry, Steve, 7–8, 10, 13

Bristol Bay, 7

Canadian Coast Guard, 23

dredges, 17

Dumping Day, 23–24, 29

Gulf of Alaska, 7, 9, 13

immersion suits, 8–9, 13

Irish Sea, 15

Jones, Gareth, 15, 17–19, 21

King, Nate, 25, 27–29

King, Ricky, 27

Kupreanof, 7–8, 10, 13

Nomada Queen, 24, 28–29

Nova Scotia, Canada, 23, 29

Ronan Orla, 15, 19

scallops, 15, 17

U.S. Coast Guard, 10, 13

winch, 17–18, 21

Yelvington, Jason, 10, 13

ABOUT THE AUTHOR

Tyler Omoth has written more than 25 books for kids, covering a wide variety of topics. He has also published poetry and award-winning short stories. He loves sports and new adventures. Tyler currently lives in sunny Brandon, Florida, with his wife, Mary.